Kieran's

Unique Short Stories For Kids

Written by

Kieran Terence Quinn

ISBN: 978-1-916820-91-3

Contents

Beeboy

Chapter 1
Riding the Bike

One day there was a boy riding his bike.

He bumped over a rock and fell off his bike. Then, he got stung by a bee.

'Oh no! I think I have shrunk,' said the boy.

'Oh no,' he said, 'I'm a bee!'

'Ha, ha!' said a bully bee. 'I have stung you. The only way to be a human again is if you go to the secret agents' base to get a potion.'

Chapter 2
The Location

Beeboy met a friendly bee, called Jeffrey. Jeffrey said he would help him.

Jeffrey gave Beeboy a watch and said, 'I will send you the location of the base on this watch.'

Beeboy followed the location on the watch and said, 'I'm at the base. Oh no, there are two guards at the entrance.'

Beeboy thought for a moment and then said, 'I have a plan.'

Chapter 3
The Plan

Beeboy said, 'I have a pen in my back pocket. I will surprise the guards and squirt the ink from my pen into their faces.'

The guards yelled, 'Augh! Oww! I cannot see! I think I hear a bee.'

Chapter 4
The Potion

Beeboy said, 'Now it is time to drink the potion.'

Beeboy drank the potion and said, 'Yes, I feel bigger. I am human again! Oops! I need to get out of here. I think I hear those guards.'

Chapter 5
Stung Again

Beeboy said, 'I am going to ride my bike home. Aughhhhhhhhhhhh! I am going to crash!'

He hears a Buzz Buzz.

Beeboy said, 'Oh no, I have become smaller. Oh no, I am a bee again!

Two hours later, 'It is okay.' The potion has worked and I am back as a human.'

The end

The Treasure Map

Chapter 1
The Map

One day, Mr Poo was with his friends Mr Wee, Cold Fart and Big Eejit. They were all at Mr Poo's birthday party at the park, with a big cake. Mr Wee went on the slide. Cold Fart went on the seesaw. Big Eejit swung on the swing.

There was also a bully called Dead Rat at the park. No one liked Dead Rat, so he played by himself.

While Big Eejit was on the swing, Mr Poo tripped over and went splat everywhere.

Mr Poo then realised he had a treasure map on his face. Mr Poo exclaimed, 'Look guys! I found a map!'

Mr Wee asked, 'How?'

Mr Poo said, 'I tripped over and found it on my face.'

Chapter 2
The Treasure Hunt in the Woods

Mr Poo turned to read the treasure map but suddenly stopped. 'Wait! Where is the treasure map? I had it in my hand a minute ago.'

Mr Wee said, 'Now what are we going to do?'

Big Eejit said, 'I took a picture of the map when you told me to look at it.'

Suddenly, they saw Dead Rat running in the distance with the map in his hand.

Dead Rat laughed and shouted, 'Ha, ha! I have the treasure map now!'

Mr Poo said, 'Never mind, we have a picture of it, thanks to Big Eejit, so we don't need to fight Dead Rat.'

Mr Poo and his friends followed the picture of the map and two hours later, they arrived in the woods at the treasure.

Big Eejit shouted, 'Yes! We are here! We found it!'

Unfortunately, Dead Rat had gotten to the treasure before Mr Poo and his friends.

But Dead Rat only found baby nappies instead of gold and silver.

Angry at this, he threw the nappies everywhere and said, 'No gold or silver treasure. Just baby nappies!' And he ran away.

So, Mr Poo and his friends found only baby nappies and what looked like a bottle of baby milk.

But the bottle of baby milk wasn't what it seemed.

Big Eejit accidentally knocked the bottle of baby milk over and the milk spilt all over the nappies.

Big Eejit just laughed, thinking it was funny because he's Big Eejit.

Mr Poo said, 'Wait, isn't that a secret potion?'

To be continued...

CLUMSY DAISY

This is a story about a girl called Daisy who is clumsy.

One day, Daisy and her family went to the park. Every time that Daisy would go on the seesaw with her brother, she would forget to hold on and would go flying into the sky and land on her head.

On Wednesday, Daisy was going to a party and was making a cake. Daisy put the baking flour in a bowel, but it went all over her clothes. When she stirred the bowel, it went everywhere in the kitchen. So, she asked her mum to do it instead.

Daisy arrived at the party holding the cake. She was very nervous, but she did not drop the cake. She is not clumsy anymore.

So, she is no longer Clumsy Daisy.

The end

Ninja Fox

Chapter 1

Once upon a time, there was a baby fox called Freddy and his dad was a ninja.

Twenty years later, Freddy had become a professional Ninja Fox and was protecting a magic emerald.

Ninja Fox had two ninja friends called Tom the Dog and Jack the Wolf.

Ninja Fox also had two enemies called Mr Mine and Mr Bob.

Twenty-one minutes later, crash! Boom! Bang!

Tom the Dog and Jack the Wolf shouted, 'Help! Mr Mine is going to kill us!'

Chapter 2

Ninja Fox said, 'Get off of my friends.'

Mr Mine laughed. 'What are you going to do?'

Ninja Fox said, 'I will show you my ninja moves with power and speed.'

Ninja Fox did his ninja moves on Mr Mine. Mr Mine shouted, 'Augh! Augh! Augh!'

As Mr Mine ran away, he said, 'I have to get to my boss. He will be happy I have the emerald.'

Chapter 3

Ninja Fox said, 'Let's follow Mr Mine to his boss's base.'

Tom the Dog said, 'But what if we get caught?'

Ninja Fox said, 'No, we won't get caught. Don't be silly. We will be okay. We can go and get the emerald back.'

Chapter 4

Ninja Fox said, 'Finally, we are here at the base.'

Tom the Dog said, 'I see the magic emerald.'

Ninja Fox said, 'I'm going to get it.'

Mr Bob said, 'What is that noise? Augh! Who punched me? Where is the emerald?'

Ninja Fox said, 'The emerald is in my hands.'

Then Ninja Fox, Tom the Dog, and Jack the Wolf ran and jumped into the car and sped away.

Mr Bob shouted, 'Go get them!'

Mr Mine hopped into his car and drove off after Ninja Fox and his friends.

Jack the Wolf said, 'Mr Mine is catching up. I have an idea we can throw Tom's ice cream at him.'

Tom the Dog said, 'No, I like my ice cream and don't want to throw it at him.'

Ninja Fox said, 'But Mr Mine might get the emerald.'

Tom the Dog said, 'Okay, I will throw my ice cream. But you have to get me another one.'

Ninja Fox said, 'Yes, okay. Throw it now!'

Tom the Dog threw his ice cream out of the window.

Mr Mine said. 'What is that coming out of their car window? Wait, it's an ice cream!'

Splat! The ice cream landed right on Mr Mine's car.

Mr Mine shouted, 'I can't see!' and had to stop his car.

Jack the Wolf said, 'Quick, go faster.'

Ninja Fox said, 'We made it back.'

Tom the Dog and Jack the Wolf shouted, 'Hooray!'

The end

Football Tips

1. When you are taking a penalty, your eyes can decide which side to go to.

2. You need to put the ball on the back of your foot to do a rainbow flick.

3. To be a good team, you must pass the ball to your team mates.

4. Make sure you have fun.

5. Work as a team.

6. Do a warm up.

7. Do football training.

8. Play football with your family so you get experience.

The end

The Couch Potato

Once upon a time, there was a lazy Couch Potato.

He often said, 'I have everything I need like cereal and milk, a toothbrush, and my dog. But I hate the sun in my eyes.'

One day, Couch Potato was watching television. While he was watching the TV, the sun was in his eyes.

Couch Potato said, 'Grrrrrr, my eyes hurt from the brightness of the sun.'

Couch Potato had a little invention. A mechanical hand that could stretch out and pull the curtains shut to block out the sun.

So, his mechanical hand stretched from the couch and closed the curtains, so there was no more sun in his eyes.
But the mechanical hand knocked over a box and it fell onto the couch.

Couch Potato did not know what was inside the box.

He opened it and found that the box was full of old photos of him and his friends.

There were photos of him and his friends sitting on a bench in the park. That was when he was not always sitting on the couch.

Couch Potato thought of all the old memories he had from when he was not always sitting on the couch.

His dog barked and barked, so Couch Potato took his dog for a long walk in the park.

So, he is not really Couch Potato anymore. He is more like Outside Potato because he goes outside every day now.

The end

The Egg

One day, I threw an egg over the wall.

Then I climbed over the wall and got the egg back.

The end

My book of short stories are unique for kids. From a boy who becomes a bee to a fox who becomes a ninja. My stories are unusual to provoke your imagination. Ideal for kids to read or anyone who just likes unique short stories. I hope you enjoy reading my stories from *Kieran, age 7.*

Milton Keynes UK
Ingram Content Group UK Ltd.
UKHW020717101123
432311UK00010B/127

9 781916 820913

Gloom 3:

subfloor intensities

GLOOM BY JAKE REBER

1111 PRESS

2024

JAKE REBER

VATICGLITCH.NET

11:11 Press

1111press.com

gloom
subfloor
intensities

ERROR

SHIMMMEEERRRR

SPLITTTTTTT

hang on tight

SPITTTTTT

(& Spit on me)

Digital undead

Possessed computers

PAGES FLASH. STATIC BENDS. ERROR SCREENS. WARNING> WARNING> WARNING. YOUR COMPUTER IS POSSESSED BY THE GLOOM. FREE URSELF. SEND THIS TO EVERYONE YOU KNOW...

PWNEJOFWPOFNWPOEN

SCCCCRRRREEEEEENNNNNNN

the screen begins to crack, split, shatter, spilllll

huumummummum

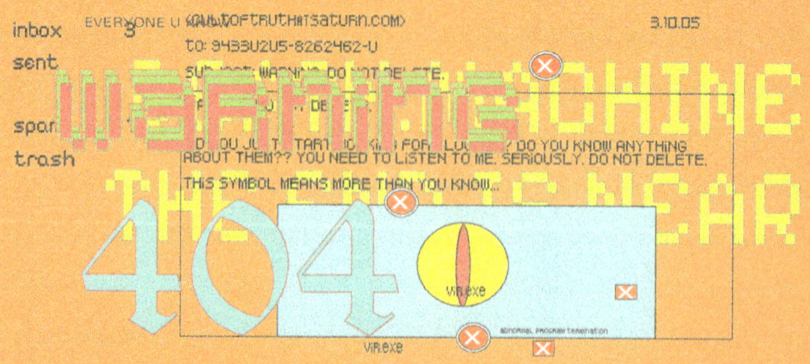

The lines etched in the screen, shattering my reflection and oozing a blue liquid, retracing the lines already adding texture and a subtle shimmer to the screen.

ERROR
TER IS POSSESSED BY THE GLOOM
TO FREE URSELF SEND THIS TO
EVERYONE U KNOW
WARNING
404
I HAVE A STRANGE DESIRE TO TOUCH THE BLUE LIQUID. I REACH OUT
The screen bleeds
Echoes of errors and 404s
Warning warning
Nothing remains
It´s all becoming substance
More & more

first through the screen down the keyboard

across the room ... creeping slowly

It begins to pool

under my fingernails.

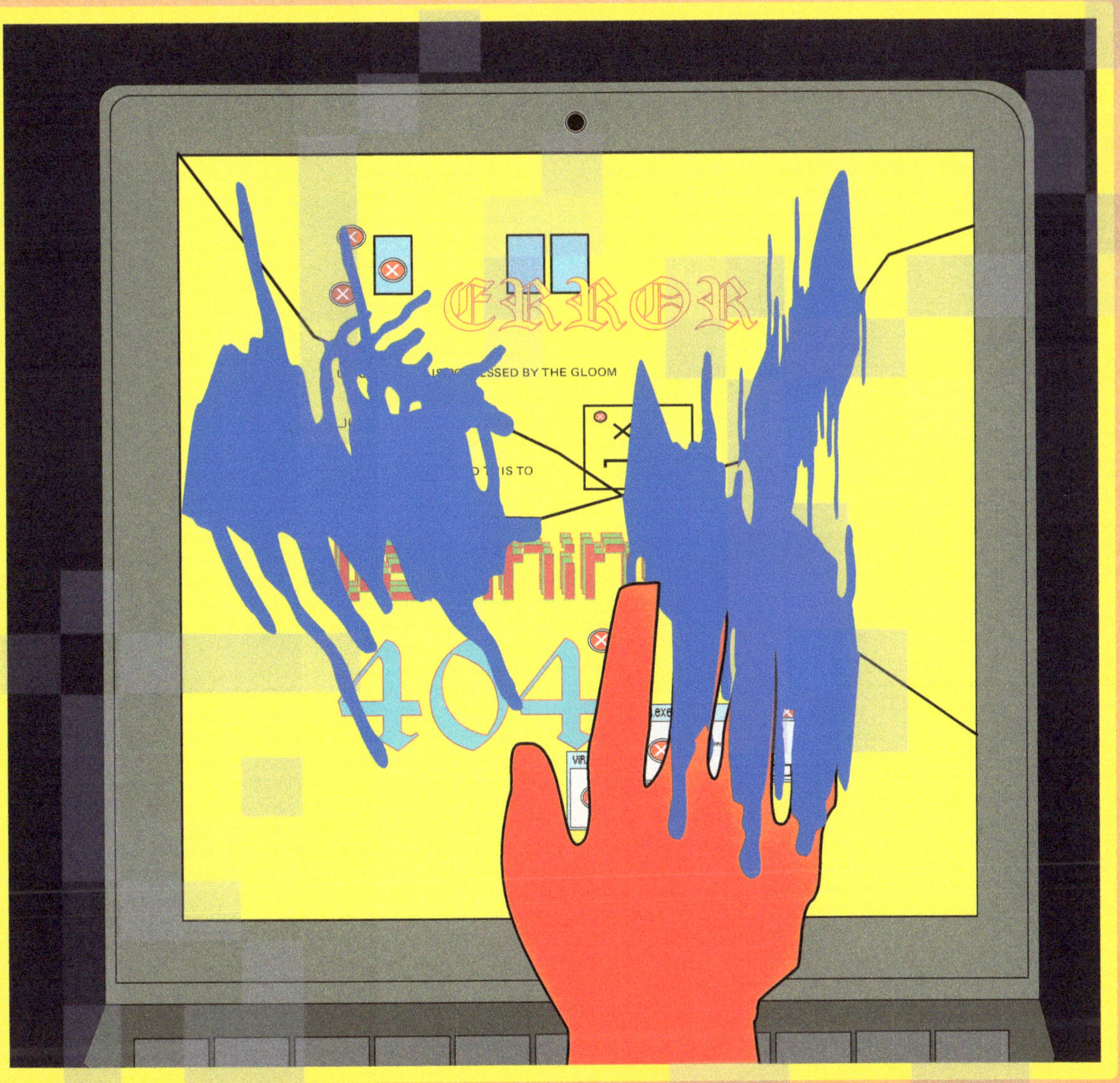

A hum.

As it spreads it forms subtle ripples and waves...
liquid crystal takes the skin...

A cool shimmering texture

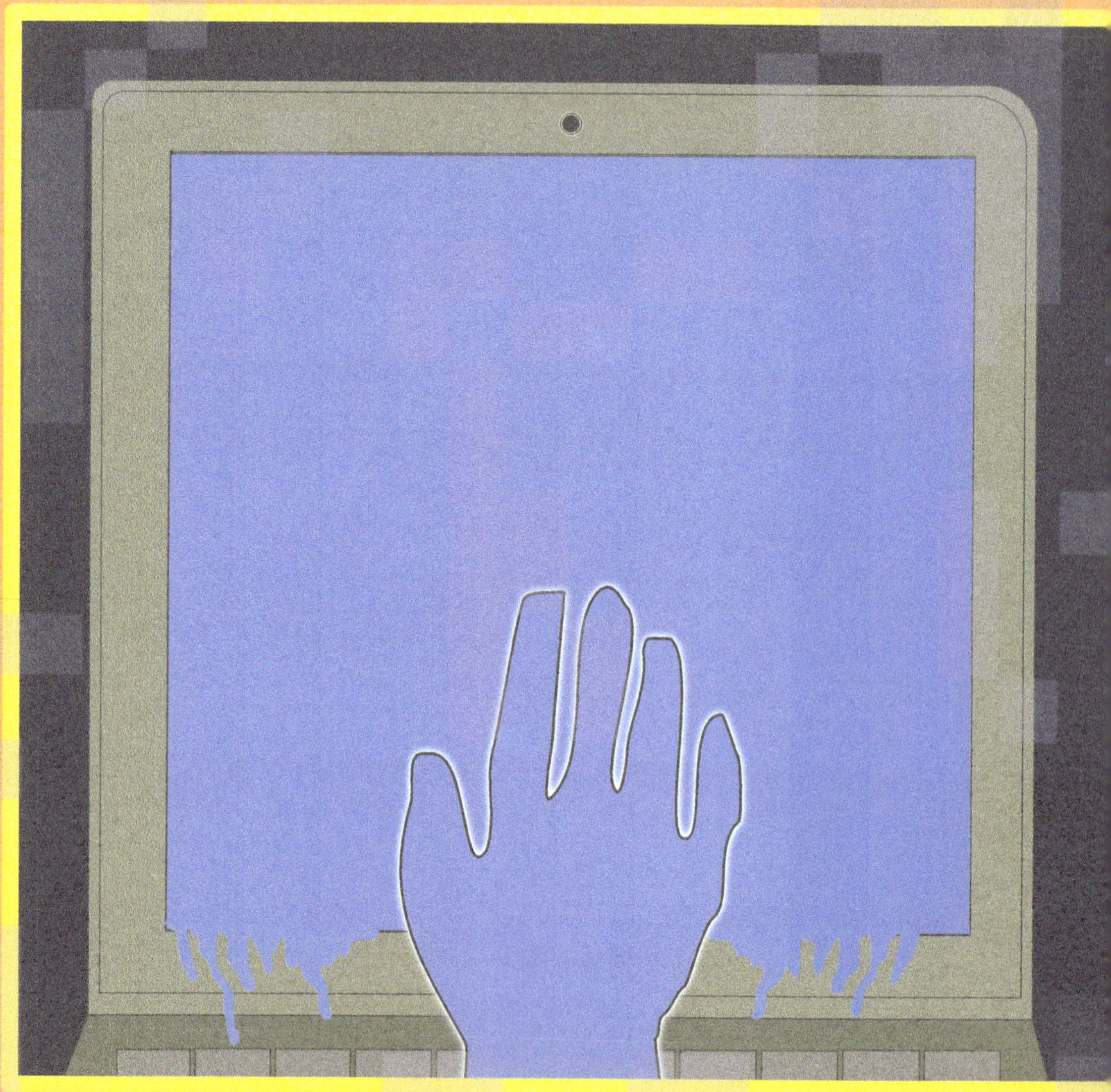

Screening the world through a living LCD. BLUE LIGHT EMBODIED>

THE SCREEN VIBRATES BLUE. THEN A SINISTER SMIRK. A SMILE APPEARS. THE SCREEN HAS ALWAYS WANTED TO EAT US ALL> SOMETIMES IT FEEDS WHEN WE BEGIN TO FADE INTO THE SCREENSPACE>

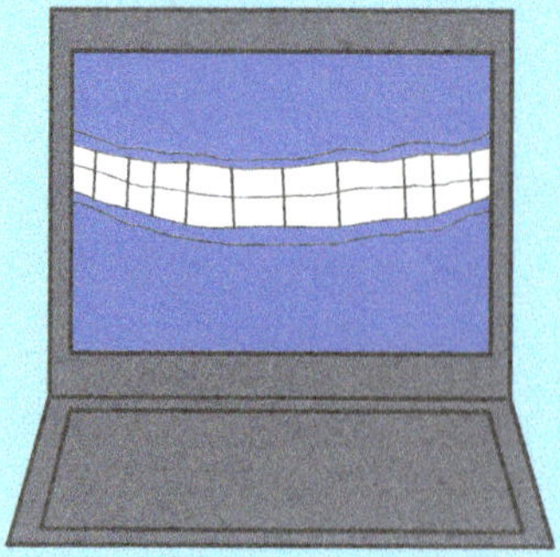

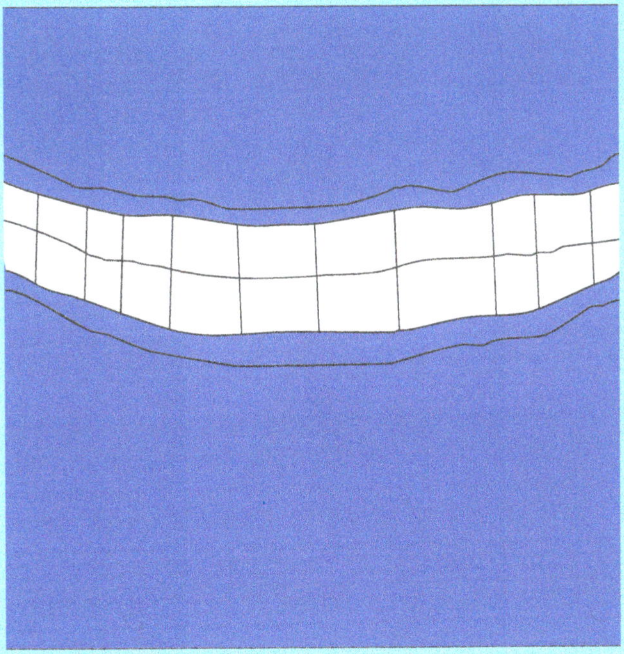

THE TEETH ARE SHARP PIXELS. AND THE STATIC BURNS. MY SKIN BECOMES THE SCREEN> IT"S A CANNIBALISTIC RITUAL. SCREENS EATING SCREENS>

MY BODY SPLAYED, DIVIDED ACROSS THE CONTINUOUS SURFACE,

LAYERS OF SKIN, FAT, FLESH – ALL SHREDDING, TURNING INTO A

HUMAN YARN, A SPOOL OF CAPILLARIES, ALL MOVING FROM THE ORGANIC TO THE DIGITAL – BECOMING SOME SORT OF CYBORG SCREEN

SHAPES AND VEINS AND EYES – A MACHINIC VISION MANIFESTED
ACROSS THE EMPHEMERAL SKIN AND LATEX>

ARMS SPLIT DOWN THE MIDDLE
LAYERS OF MUSCLE EXPOSED
AND THEN BLEND INTO THE
SKELETAL STRUCTURE
DRIFTING INTO THE VEINS
AND ARTERIES... ALL SHIFTING
GRADUALLY IN SUBTLE
GRADIENTS... ALL
VISUAL AND TACTILE
VARIATIONS

A transcoded body

I move deeper into the digital void

Am I still here? Did I ever leave the gloom center? Am I one with the computer?

Is this artificial intelligence? AM I A RAT? DID THEY EMBED THESE AS MEMORIES IN MY MIND?

The questions blur through my hard drive

ARTIFICIAL INTELLIGENCE
DIGITAL INHUMANITY

MY VISION EXISTS ON THE EDGES OF MY BODY<
AT TIMES IT SEEMS TO STRETCH OUT BEYOND
IT ON TINY PIXEL THREADS, WHERE THE SKIN
EXTENDED IN THINNER STRIPS, ALMOST
BECOMING TRANSPARENT...

MY TEETH START AS PIXELS TOO, BUT THEN THEY BLEED INTO THE LIQUID POOLS THAT MAKE UP WHATEVER REMAINS OF ME.

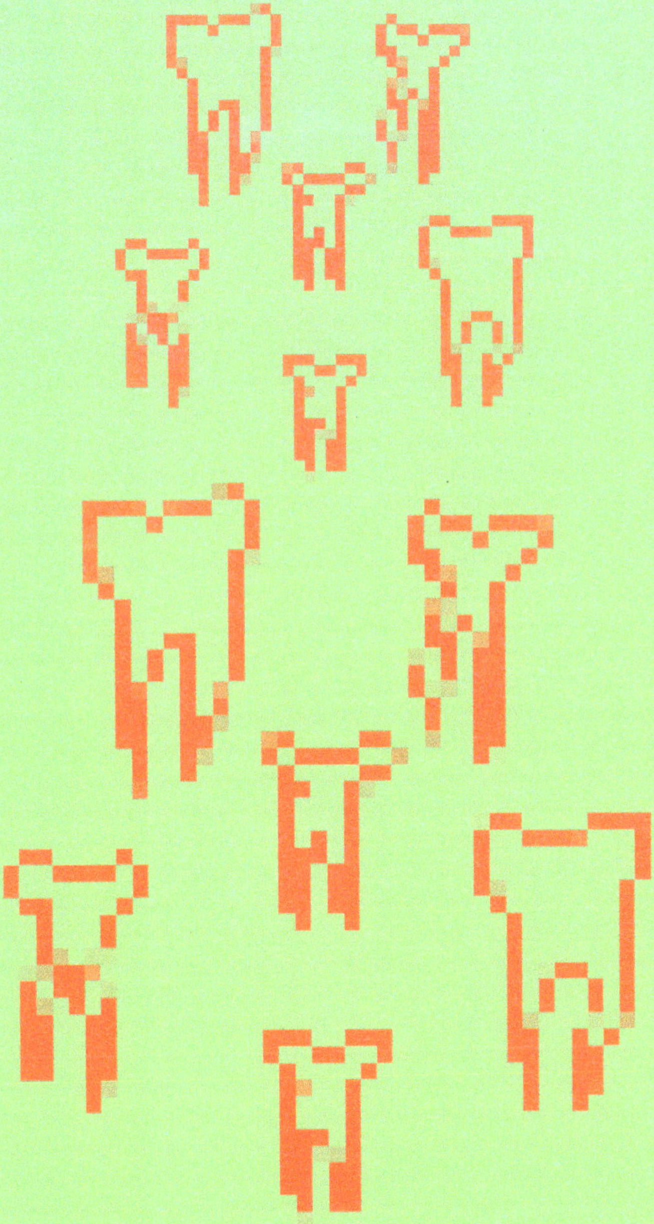

DEFANGED & BLISSED

INTO THE UNKNOWN I WANDER. A FORMLESS FORM WITHIN AN IMMATERIAL LANDSCAPE> A NON_SPACE_SITE > AN EXTENSION OF THE FLUID SCREEN> A WARPED VISION > TACTILE AND TENDER AND UNREAL

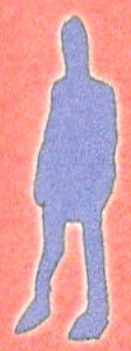

MY SIGHT BECOMES A PROJECTILE,
A DIGITAL VISION, A CEREMONY.

A MONOLITH. A PRAYER. A CHANT>

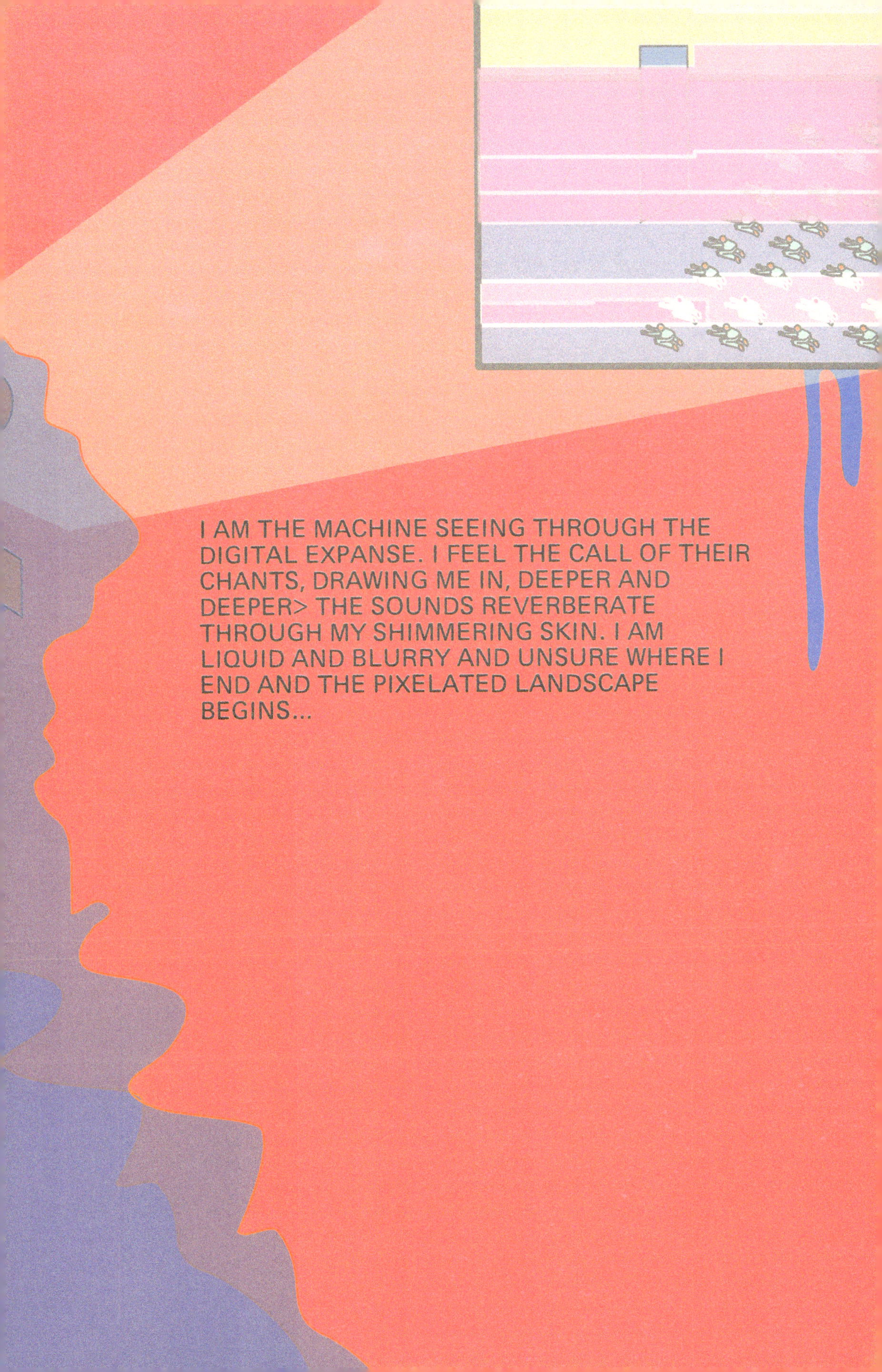
I AM THE MACHINE SEEING THROUGH THE DIGITAL EXPANSE. I FEEL THE CALL OF THEIR CHANTS, DRAWING ME IN, DEEPER AND DEEPER> THE SOUNDS REVERBERATE THROUGH MY SHIMMERING SKIN. I AM LIQUID AND BLURRY AND UNSURE WHERE I END AND THE PIXELATED LANDSCAPE BEGINS...

I FEEL A TUG AT MY SPINE. AM I WIRED IN? ARE THOSE GLOOM VISIONS PART OF THE CYBORG NETWORK? THESE SENSATIONS ARE GLITCHED TO THE EDGE OF POSSIBILITY.
& IT FEELS BOTH REAL AND UNREAL
EACH MOVEMENT VIBRATES ACROSS MY SKIN. THE SLIPPAGE BETWEEN FEELING LIKE ELECTRICITY AND WATER AND THEN TOTAL INTENSITY

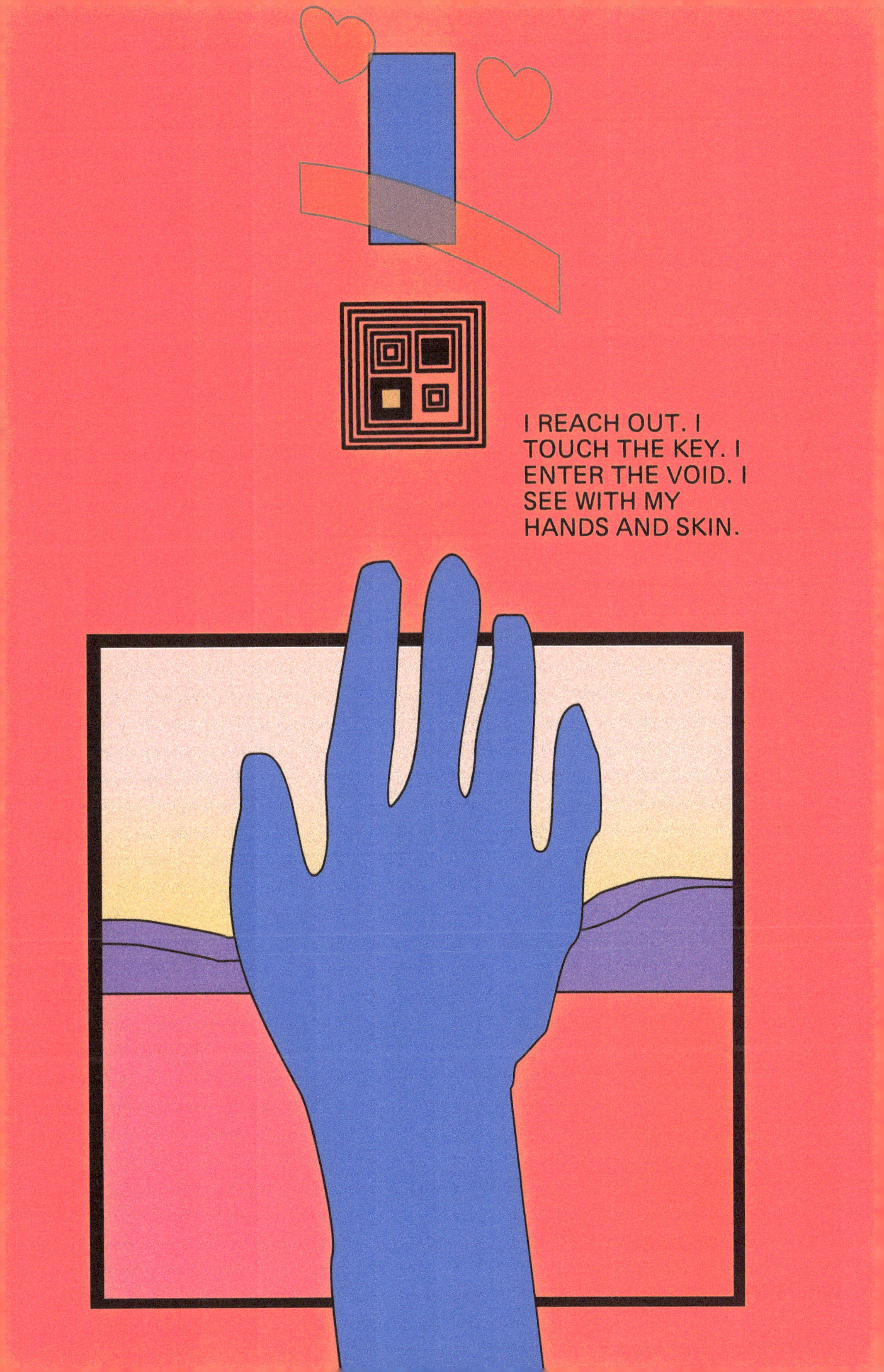
I REACH OUT. I TOUCH THE KEY. I ENTER THE VOID. I SEE WITH MY HANDS AND SKIN.

THE GLOOM APPEARS ON THE MONOLITH. THE FACELESS APPARITIONS OR HUMANS OR CYBORGS ALL PROSTRATED. THEY BOW. THEY CHANT IN A LOW RYTHMIC HUM. IT SOUNDS LIKE STATIC> THEN LIKE THE TONES OF DIALUP. THEN SILENCE.

IT BEGINS TO GLITCH. THE SCREEN OOZES> IT SPILLS AND DROOLS SEPARATING MY VISION AND FINGERTIPS> THE WIRES ARE WET>

VISUAK
!!!VIS.ERROR

ROROOROOO
NTAL INHUMANITY

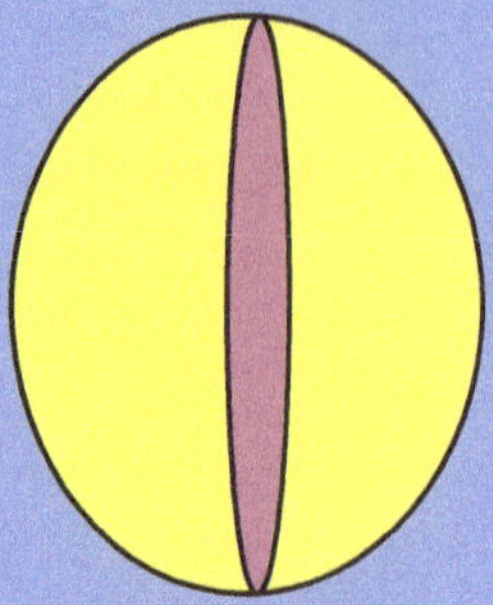

ALL THAT REMAINS IS THE EYE AND MY DIGITAL FACE – THE TRACES OF VISION AND FEELING. A CEREMONY REPLAYS IN MY INTERNAL MEMORY. I TRANSCRIBE THESE MEMORIES WITHIN. DISTRIBUTION OF THE GLOOM. IT IS NOW TIME> I MUST....

OBSERVE> FEEL> TRANSCRIBE> REFLECT> REPEAT

OBSERVE> FEEL> TRANSCRIBE> REFLECT> REPEAT

OBSERVE> FEEL> TRANSCRIBE> REFLECT> REPEAT

MESSAGES (2)
VLVTG3033: THIS IS THE WRONG TIME.
VLTVG3033: DEATH IS CLOSE
Aa Aa B U I [] LINK
VELVET? |
...
SEND

Milton Keynes UK
Ingram Content Group UK Ltd.
UKHW052242250424
441678UK00004B/39

9 798869 295378